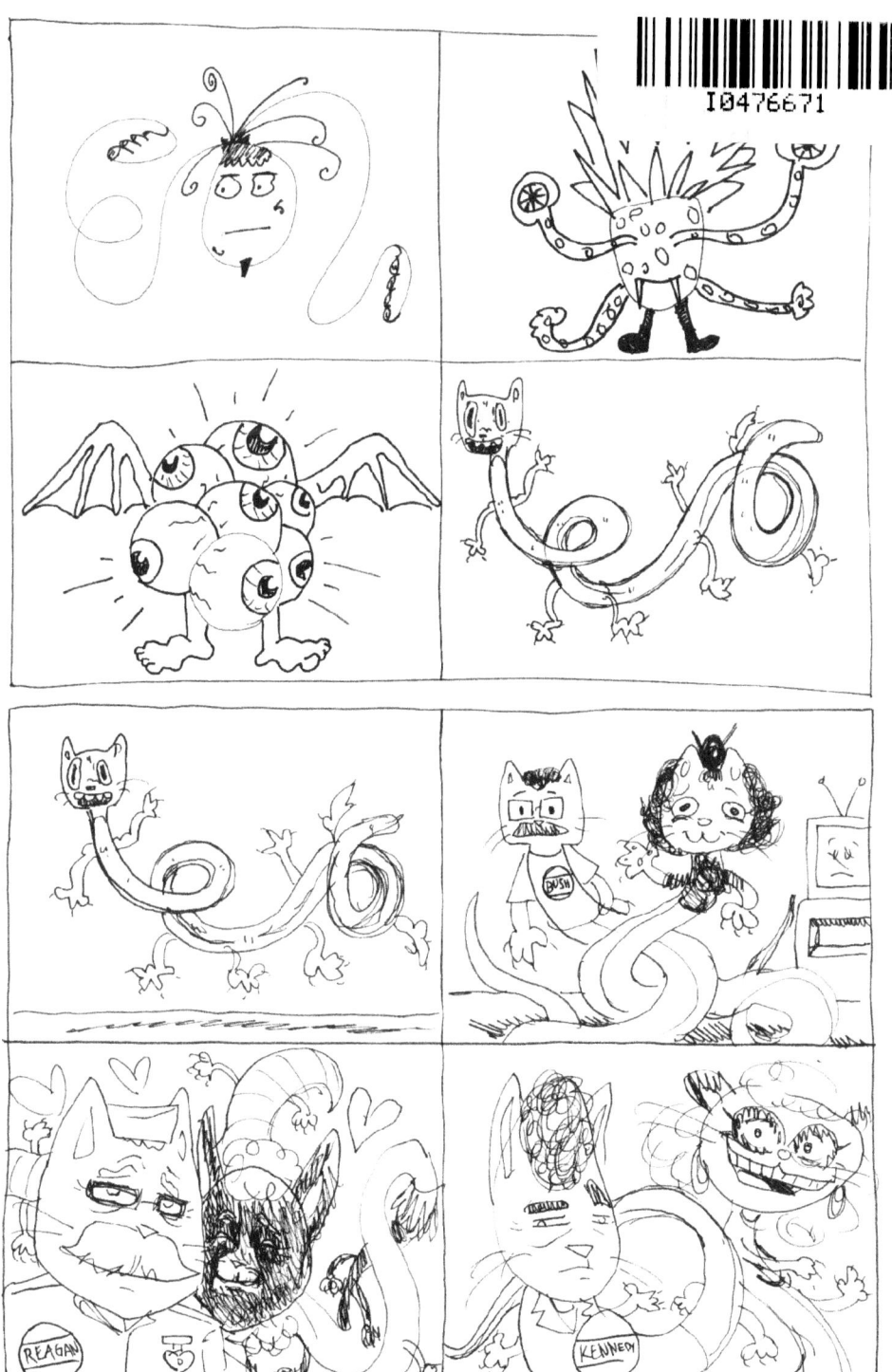

Special thanks to my classmates in the Fall 2014 Making Comics Workshop, who helped bring this character to life through our collaborative drawing jam.

MY YOUT'FULL DAYS:

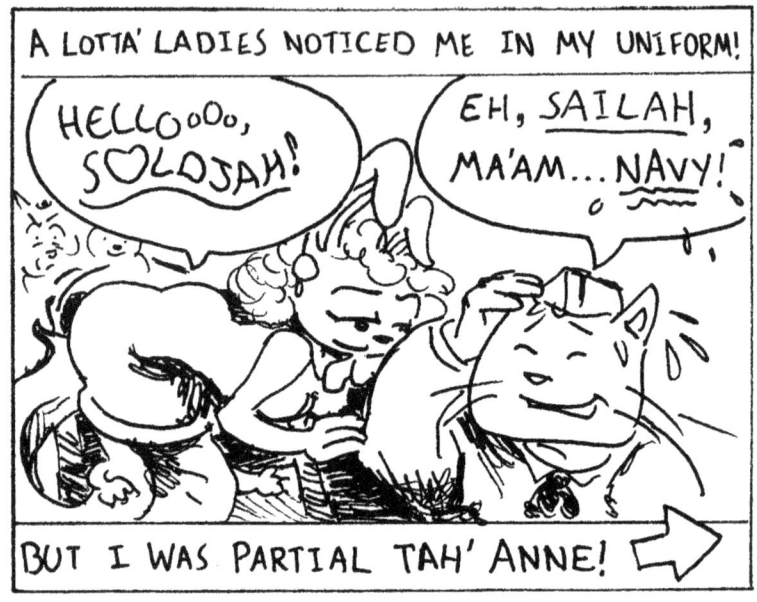

TH'DEPRESHIN' HAD BEEN HAHD ON ANNE'S FAMILY...

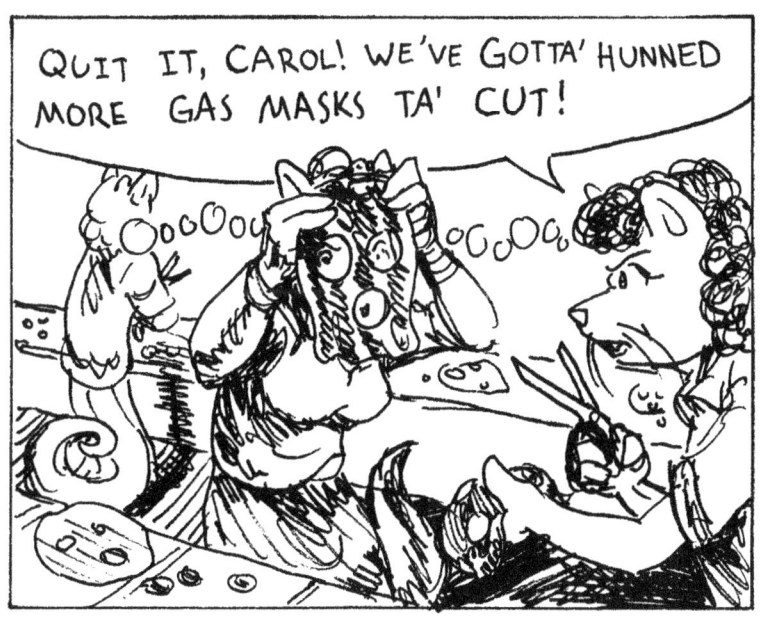

SHE CUT HOLES IN LEATHA'
AT TH' GAS MASK FAC'TRY!

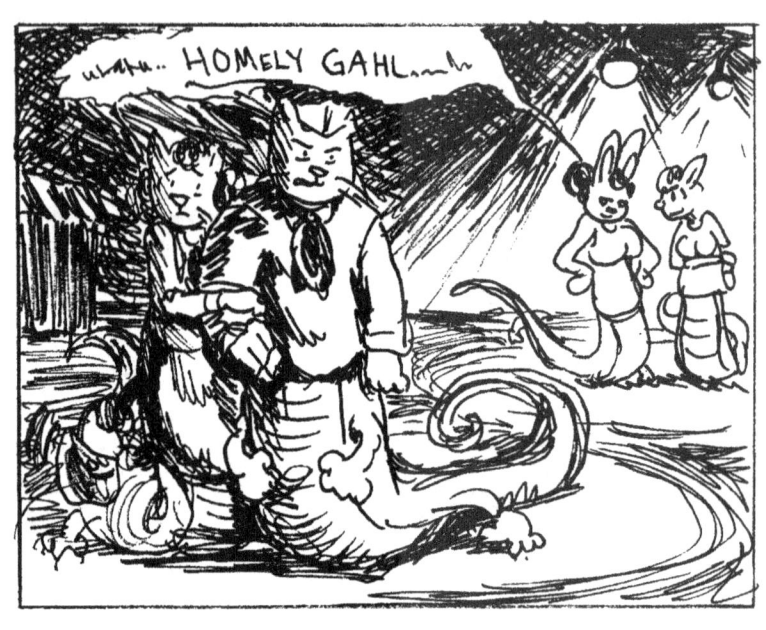

IT WAS FREQUENTLY REMAHK'D
THE TWO'VE US MADE A
QUEEAH COUPLE!

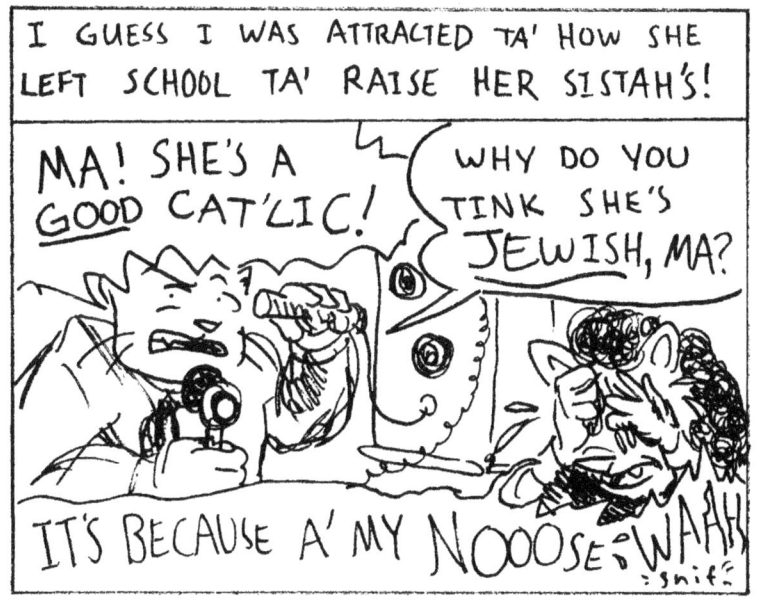

MAH FREQUENTLY, IT WAS
REMAHK'D SHE WAS JEWISH.

ONE EVENIN', WHILST BEIN' TA'GETHAH,

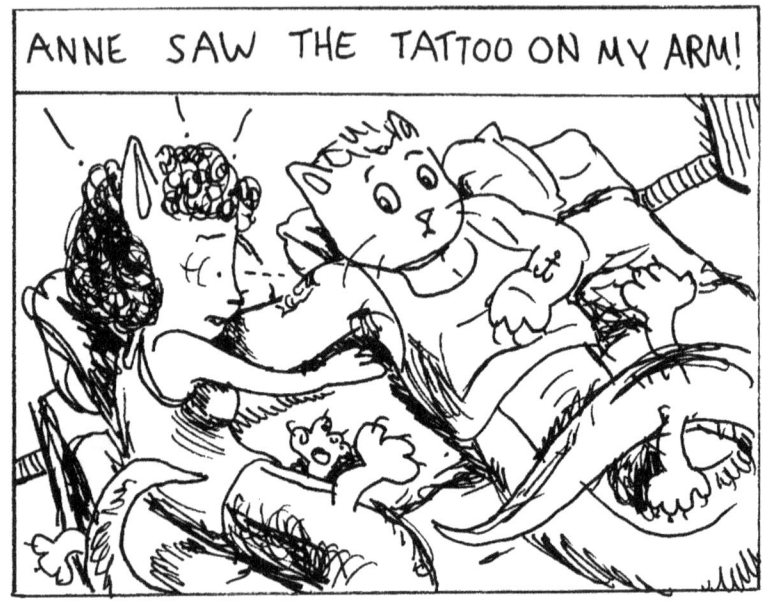

AN' SHE WAS <u>NOT</u> AMUSED...

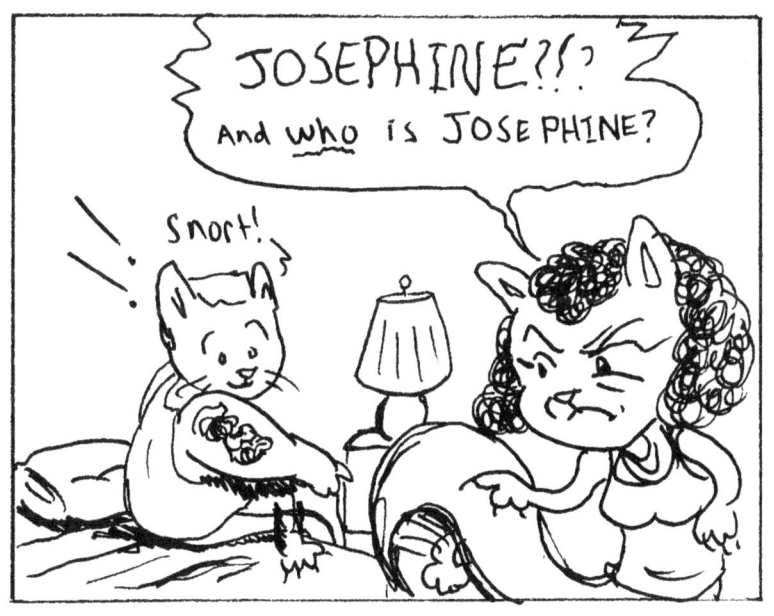

OH, ANNE!!!

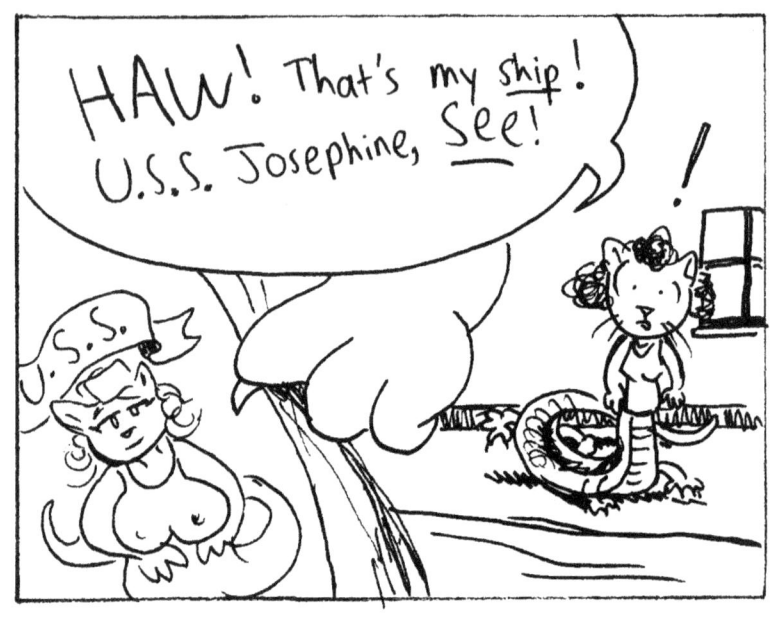

THE TAT'S GONE SPLOTCHY AN'
SOFT, NOW...

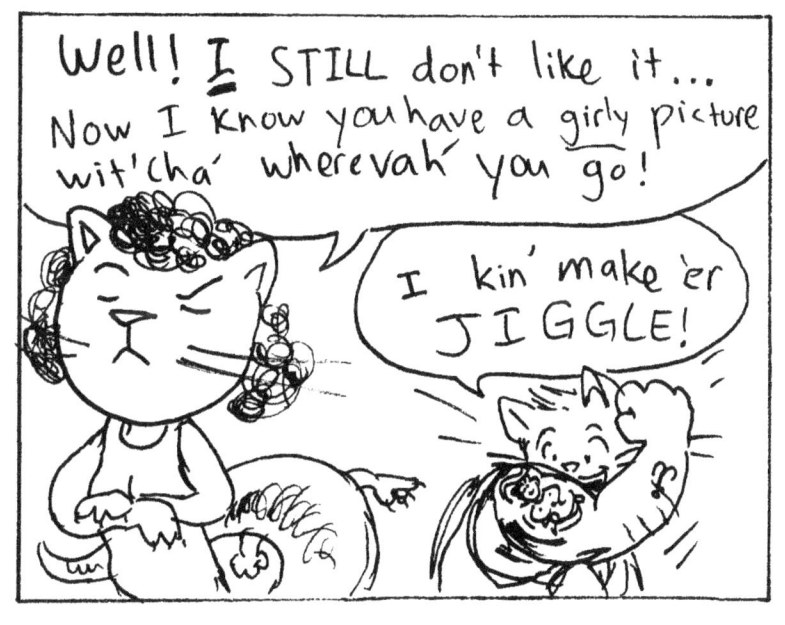

I WAS SLOW IN LEAHNIN'
TH' LANGUAGE A' WIMIN!

BLESS HER HEAHT,

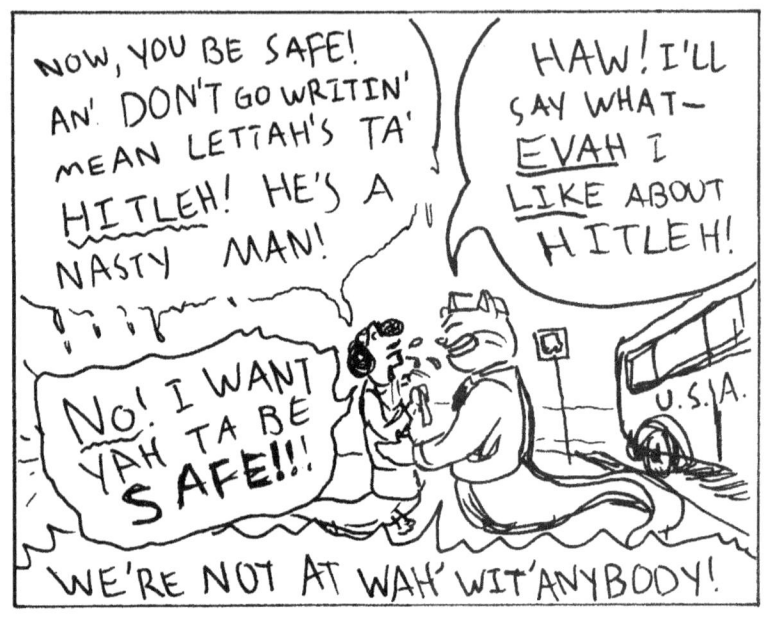

ANNE WAS PRONE TA'
WORRY'EN ABOUT NAHTHIN'!

I WUZ LOST IN THOUGHT, WEN~

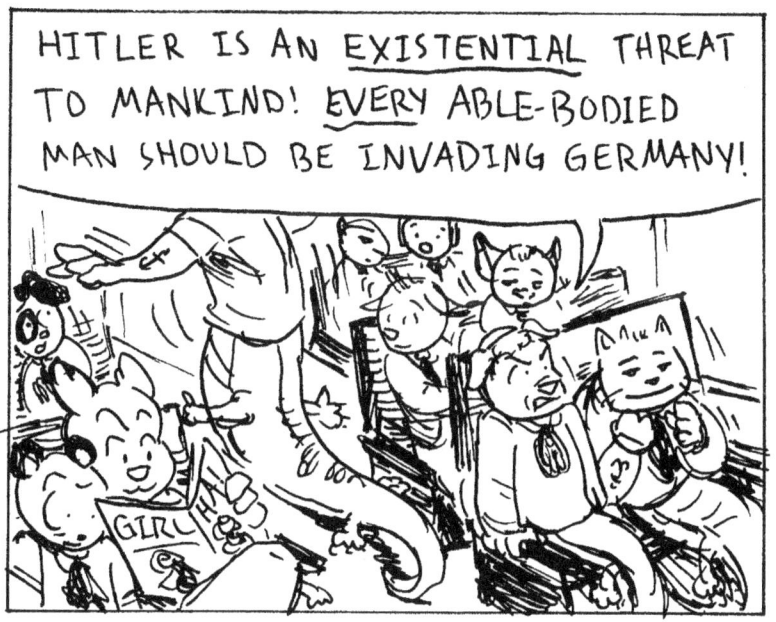

AHHHHHHHHH, ANNE!

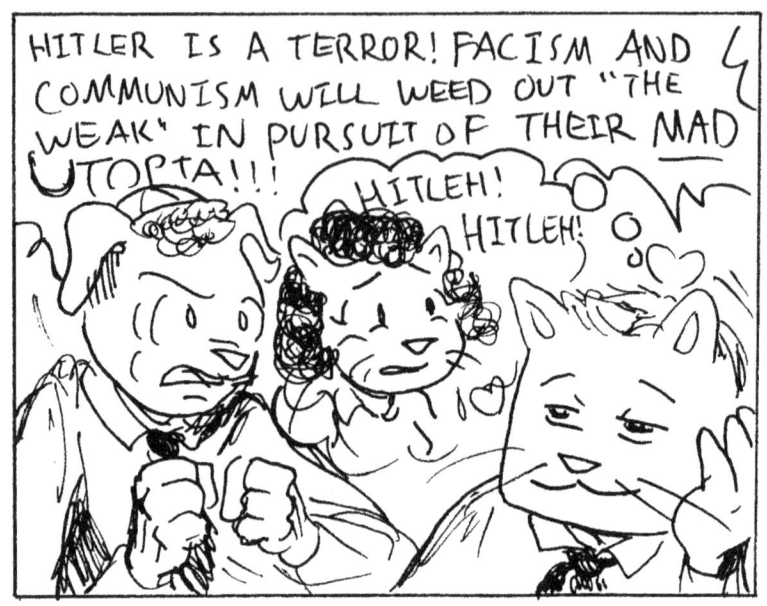

ANNE, ANNE, SWEET FRETTIN'
ANNE

OH, DAT'S HOW I MET RED!

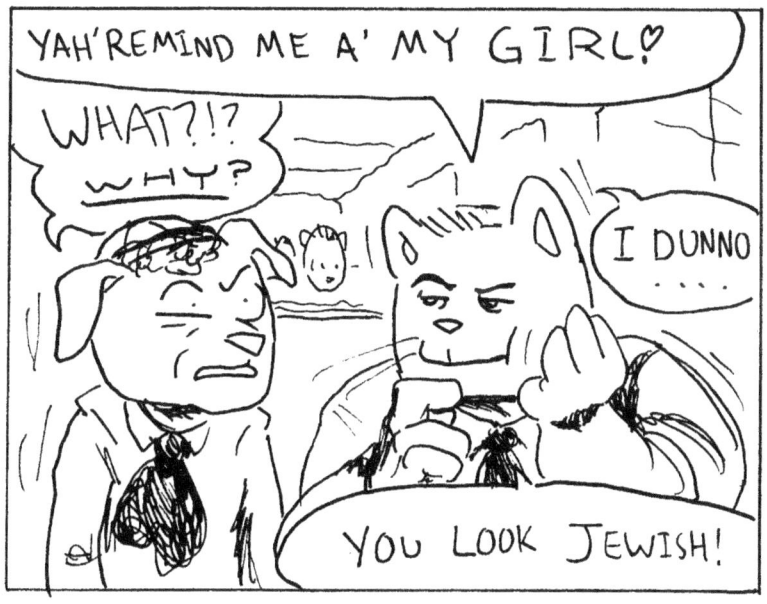

WE HIT IT OFF RIGHT AWAY!

IN HAWAII-AH, WE GOT OUR R&R.

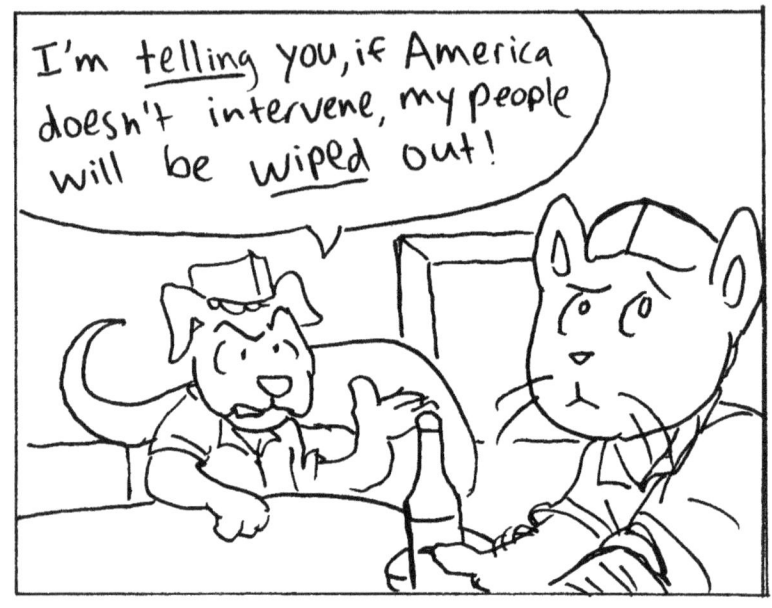

OUR DISCUSHIN'S MAINLY
CONSISTED A' RED DISCUSSIN'
BOOKS N' PHIOSOPHY AN' ME
NODDIN'!

BUT IT WAS FACINATIN' ANYHOW!

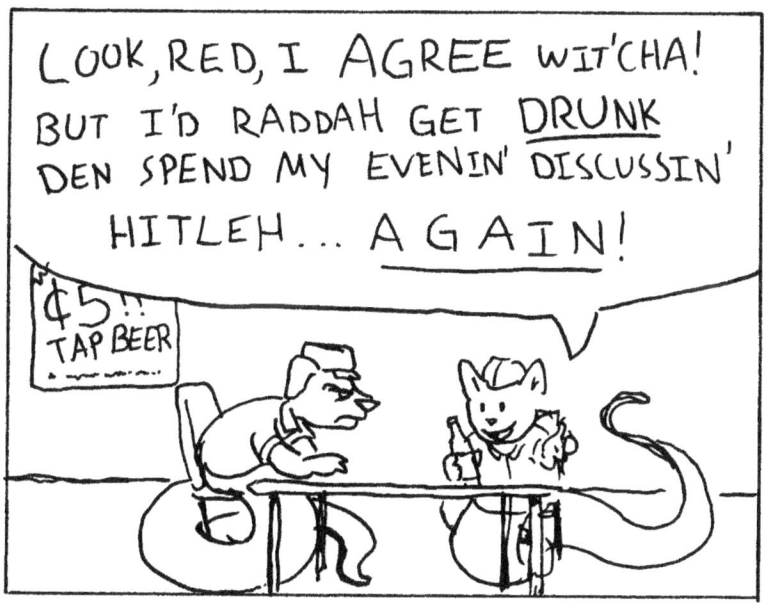

OF COURSE, I DID'N GET
DRUNK FA' ANNE'S SAKE!

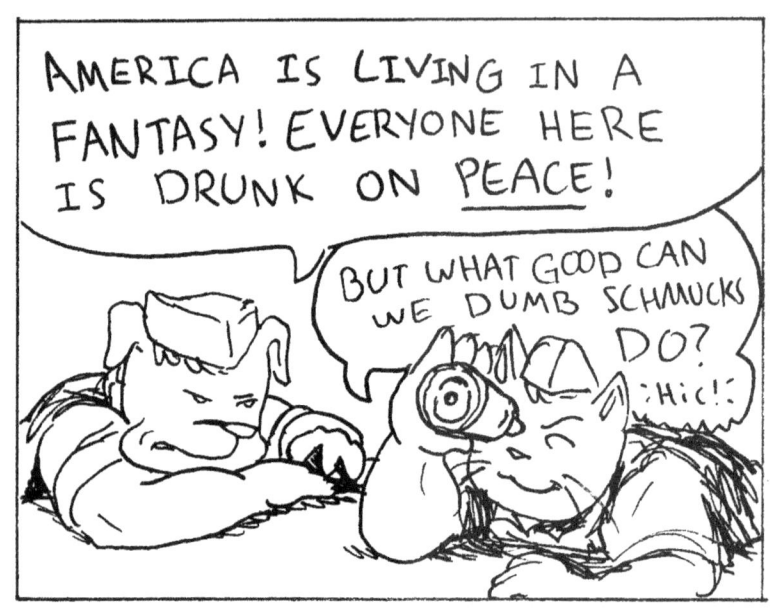

WELL, ONE OF US WAS A DUMB SCHMUCK...

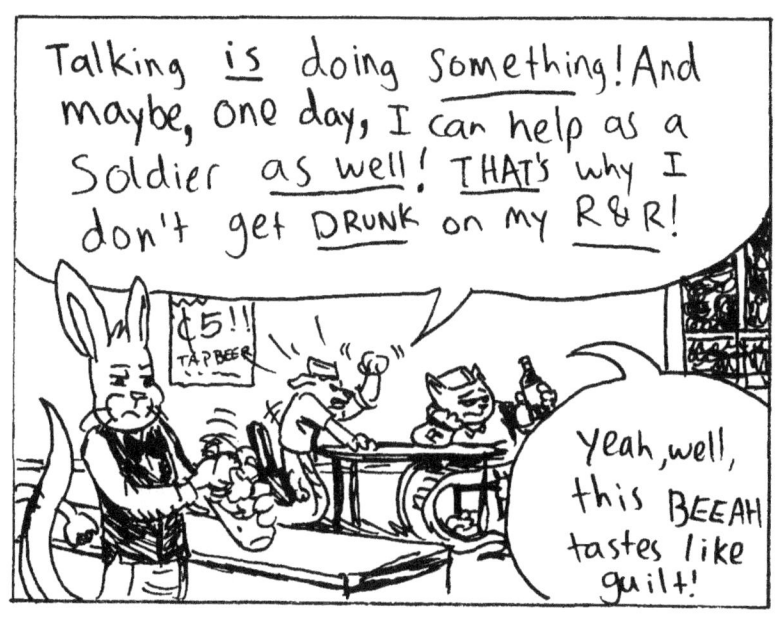

RED ALSO ENCOURAGED ME
TA' CHECK MY INK'LIN'S...

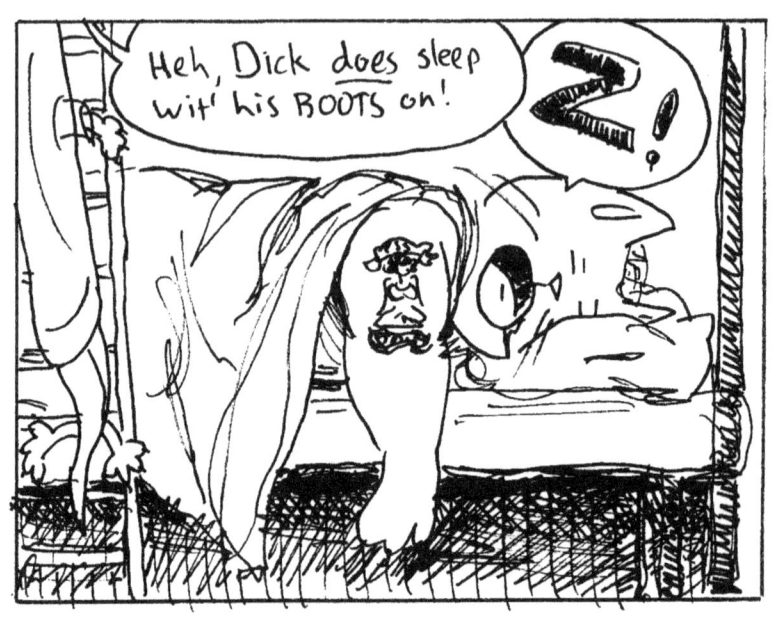

TA' THE POINT WHERE I
ADOPTED HIS HABITS OF
CONSTANT PREPAHRATION!

MY RUDE AWAKENIN':

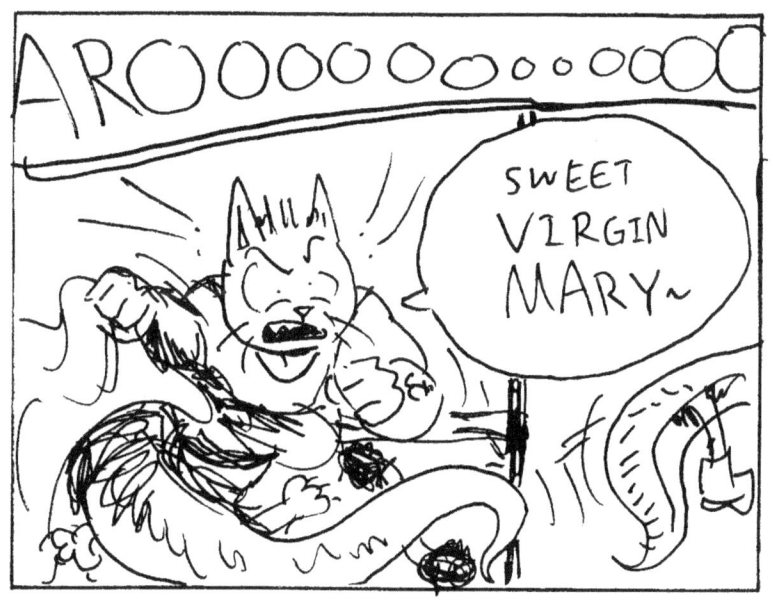

I UTTAH'D   OTHAH   WORDS
I WON'T REPEAT   HEAH...

PROB'LY ANOTHA' DRILL!

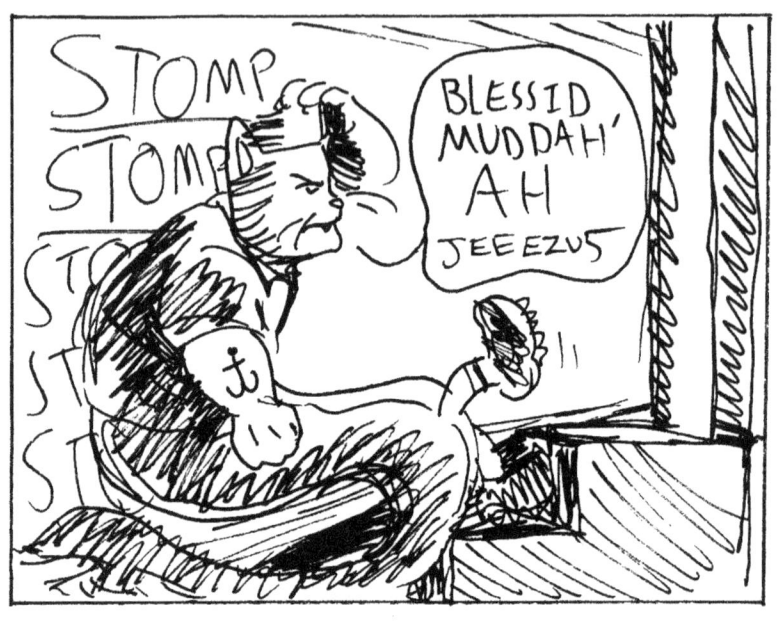

I JUS' KNEW IT WAS A DRILL!

I . . .

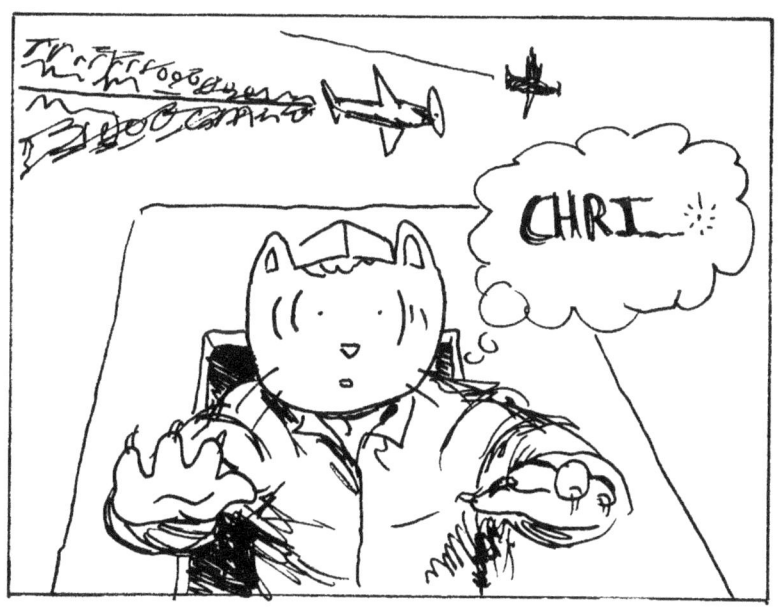

I . . .

WAS

WRONG!

CAN'T   THINK

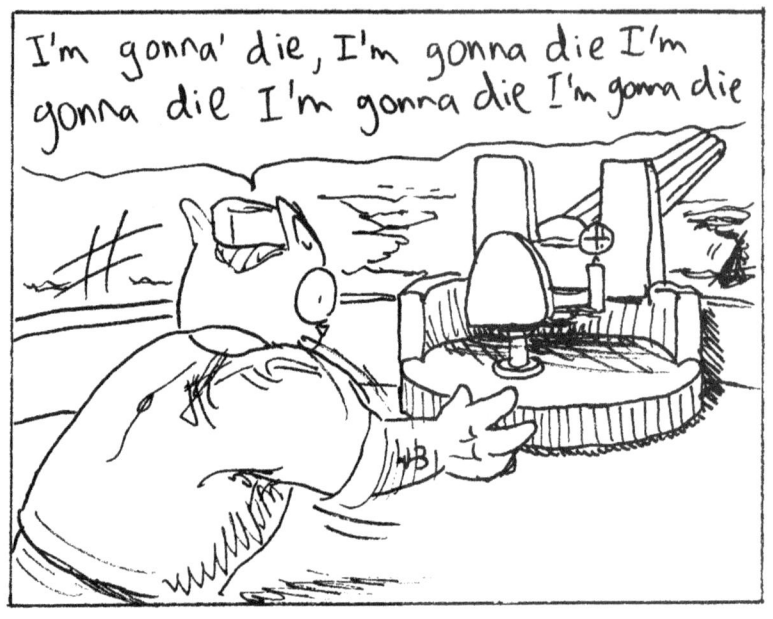

NO!   THINK   YOU'VE TRAINED
                       FER'THIS!

YER' GONNA' DIE, DICK.

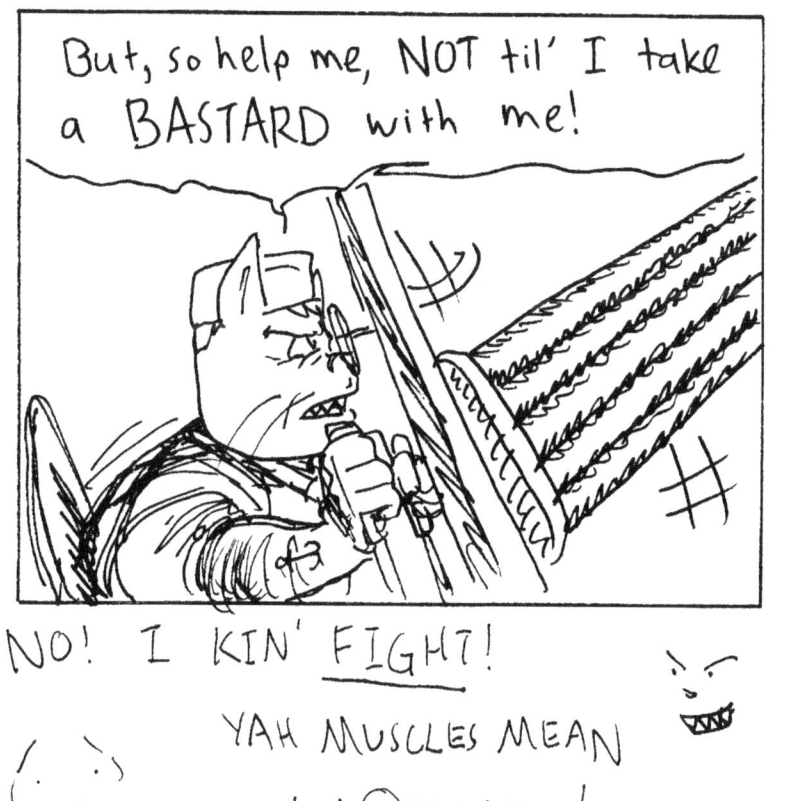

NO! I KIN' FIGHT!

YAH MUSCLES MEAN

NOTHIN' NOW...

TAKE 'EM WITH ME!

YAH DO REALIZE...

WE 'AH SITTIN' DUCKS...

WE'AH FAT, METAL,

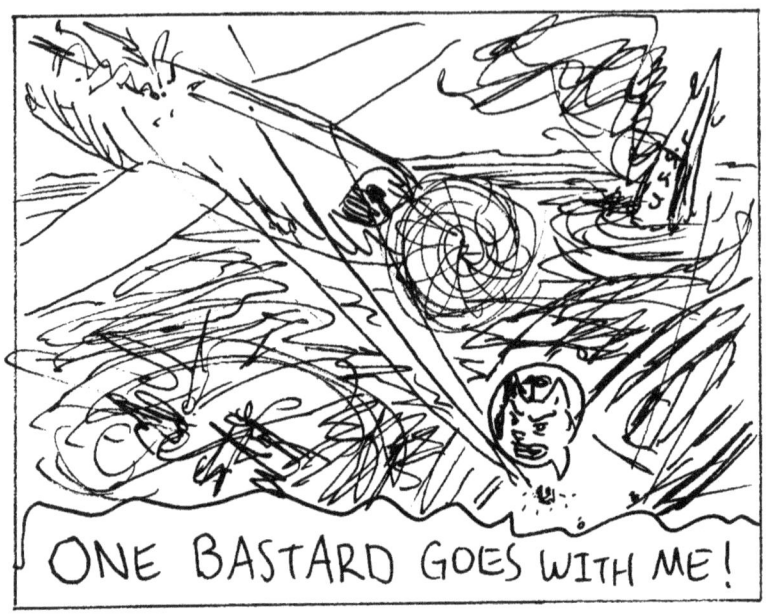

SITTING, DUCKS,

NO NO NO NO NO NO NO NO NO NO NO NO

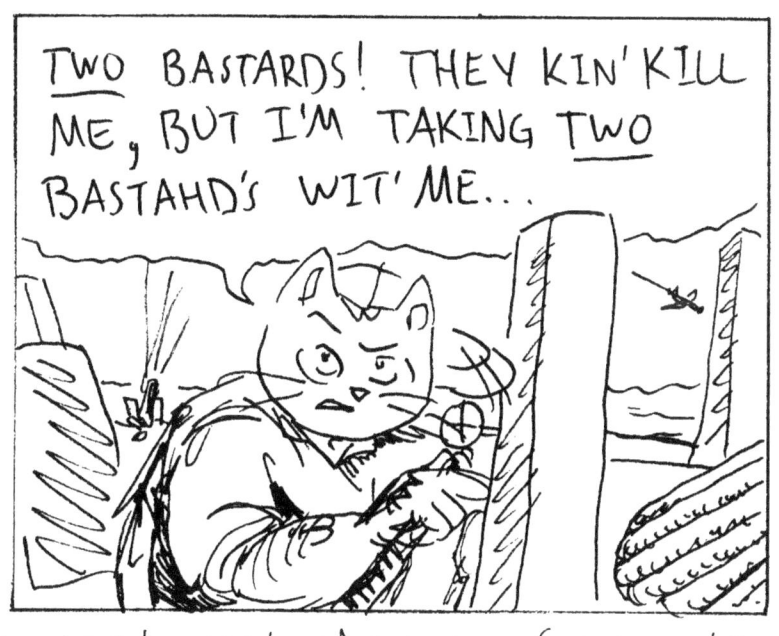

WHAT'S MY MOUTH SAYIN'?

LIVE ! KILL! KILL!
. KILL! KILL!
FIGHT ! KILL! KILL!
' KILL! KILL!
WIN ! KILL! KILL!
KILL! KILL! KILL! KILL! KILL!
KILL! KILL! KILL! KILL! KILL!

THE SUN IS RISIN'

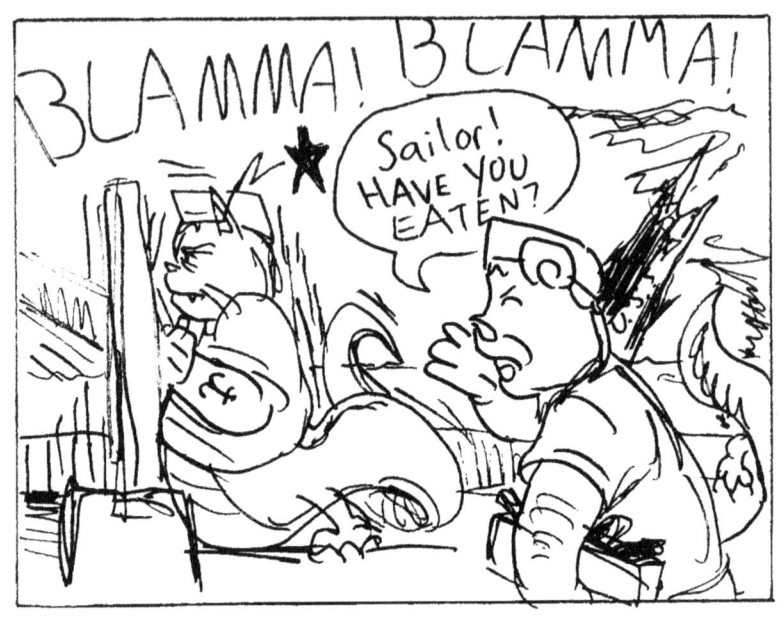

RISIN' SUN... WHO AH' THEY?

WHOEVAH YOU AH'...
BURN IN
HELL!

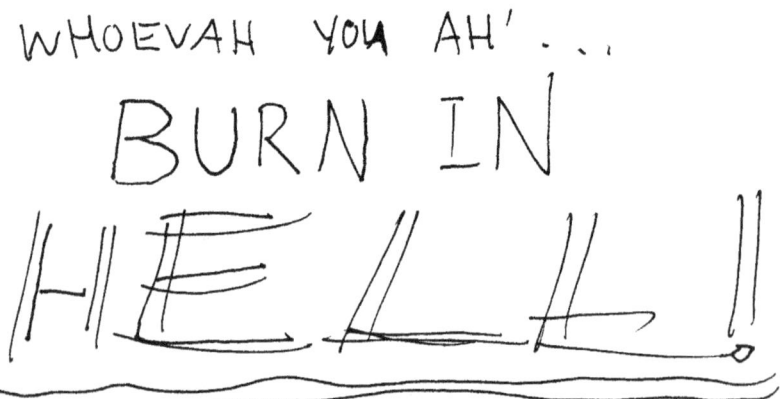

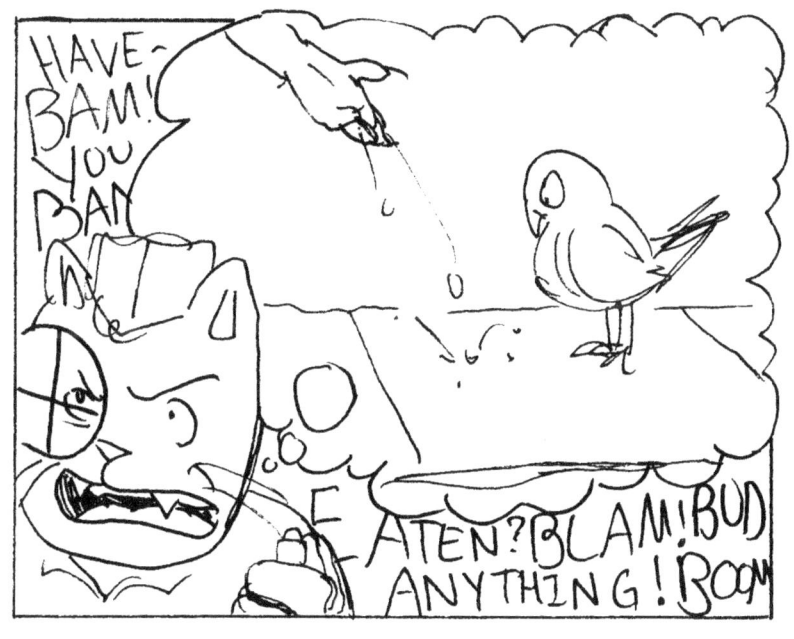

FEAH. FAT. SITTING DUCKS.

BIHD. SCARED BIHD.

FOOD. FRIGHTENED.

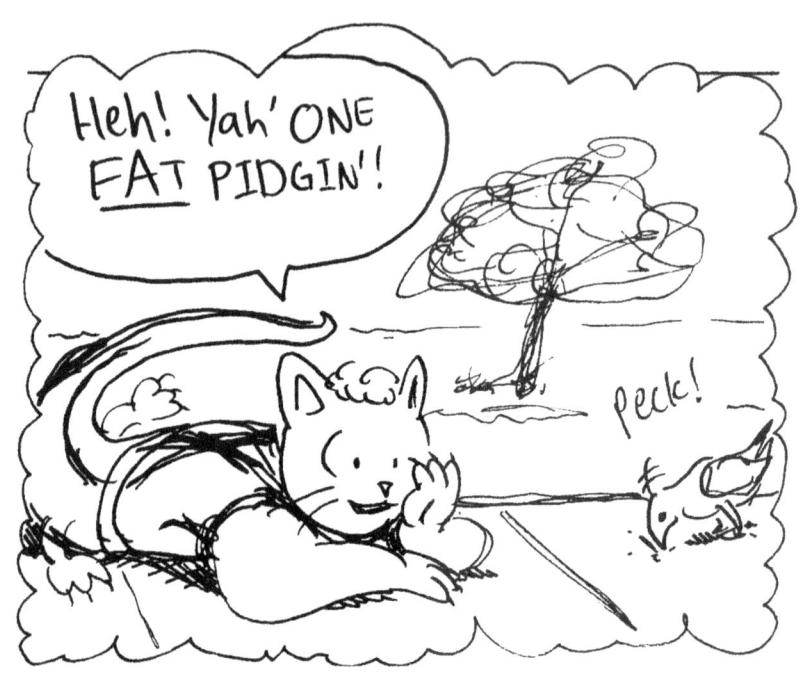

YAH' ONE TA' TALK.

SURPRISE! FEAH! DEATLY FEAH!

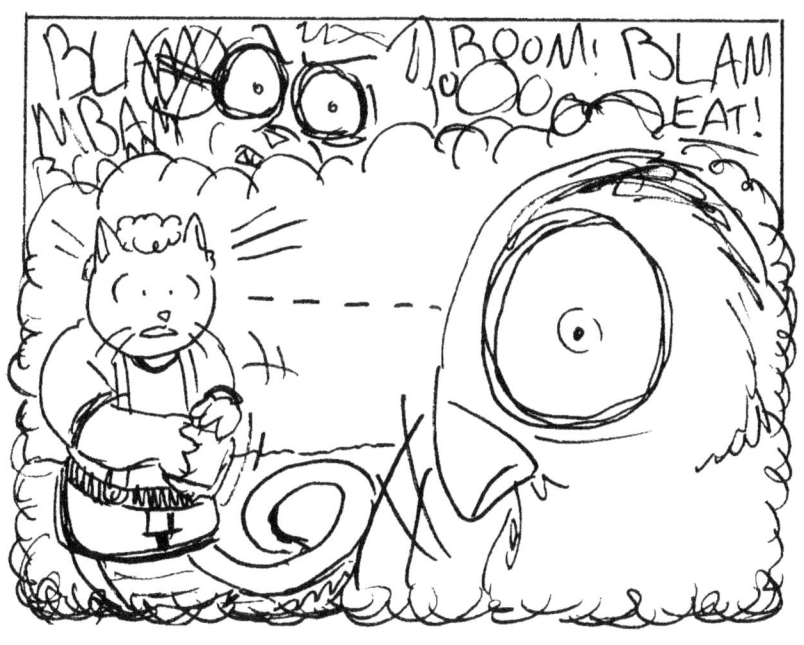

CORNER'D! TRAPPED! FAT!
FOOL! WHY? FOOL. FOOD!
HUNGER. HUNT. DEATH, JESUS?

WHY DO I HAVE...

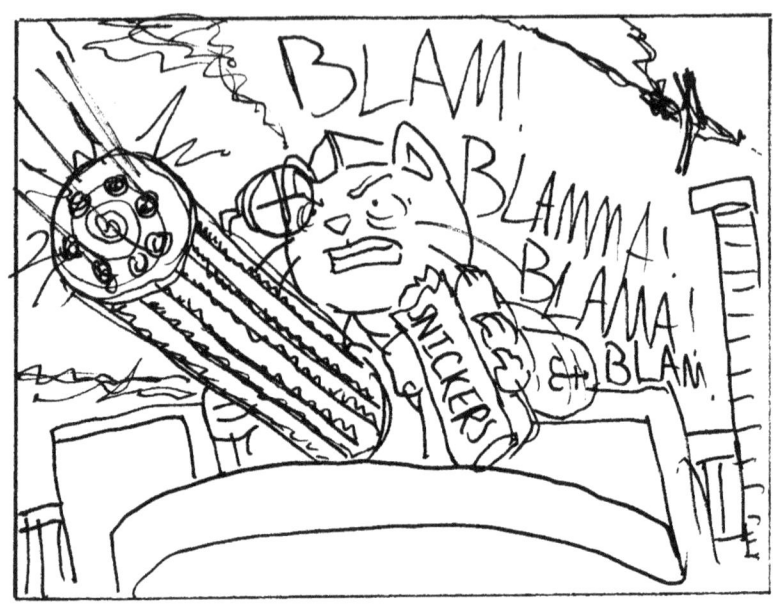

A SNICKAH'S BAH?

THE SNICKERS IS ALL I EAT...

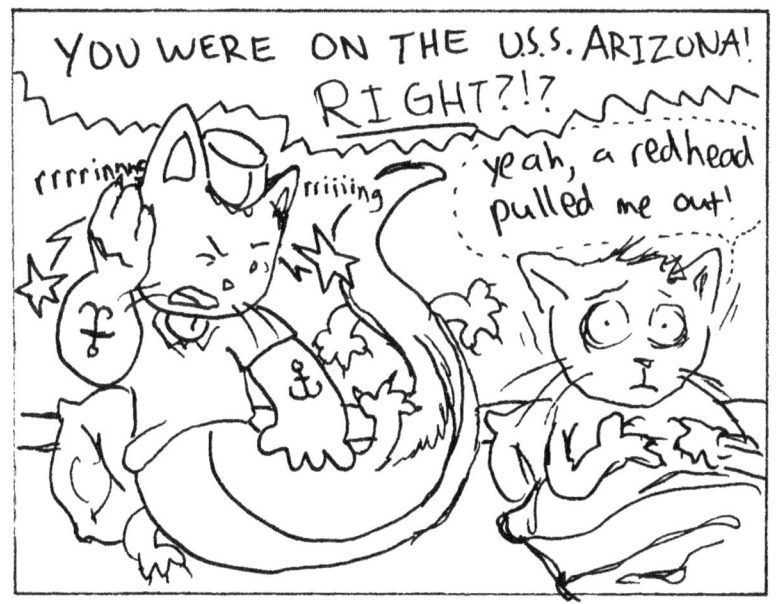

UNTIL IT IS OVAH...

WHY AM I TALKIN' SO QUIET??

RED?!? JESUS!?!

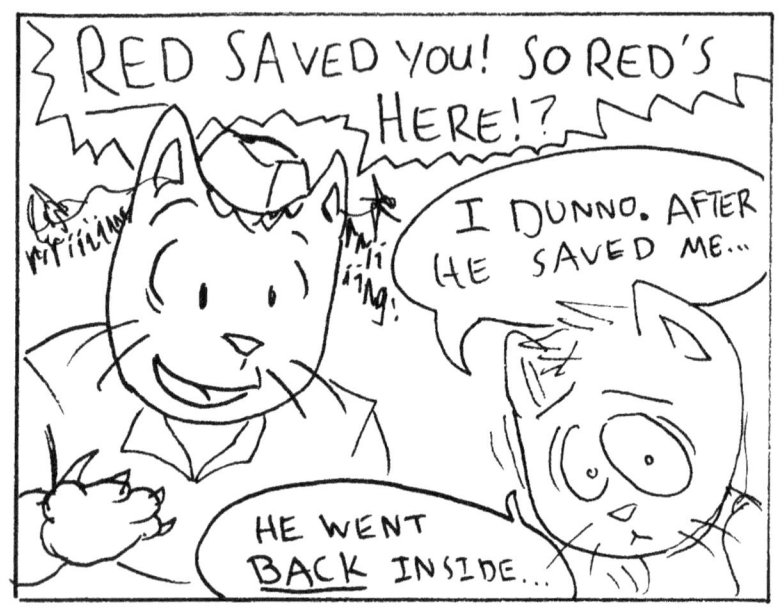

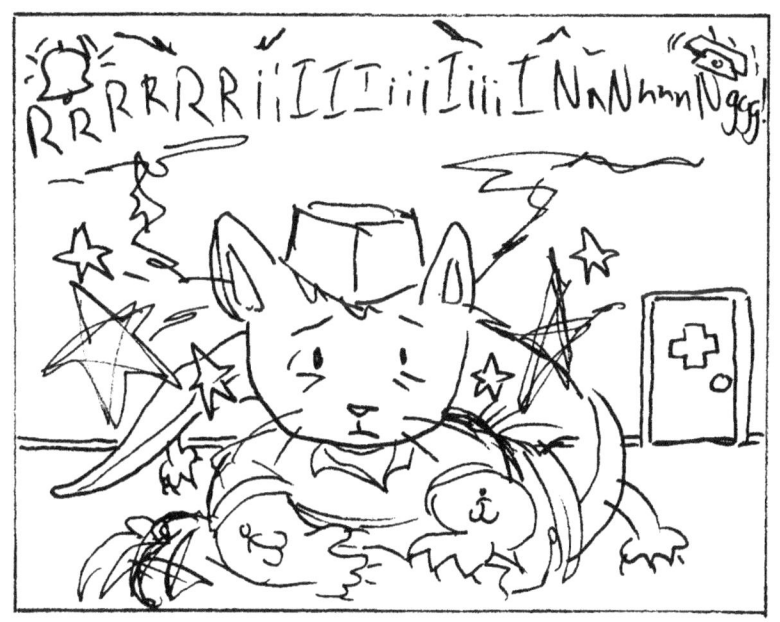

RED?

JESUS.

THEY SAY I NEED R&R!

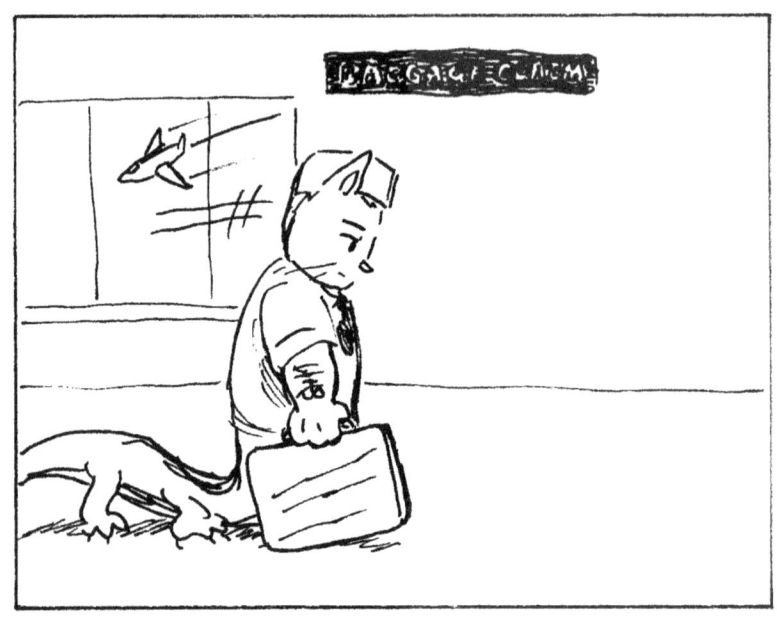

I'M NOT FINISHED. IT'S WAH
NOW. I'LL BE BACK THEAH.
BUT FAH NOW, REST...

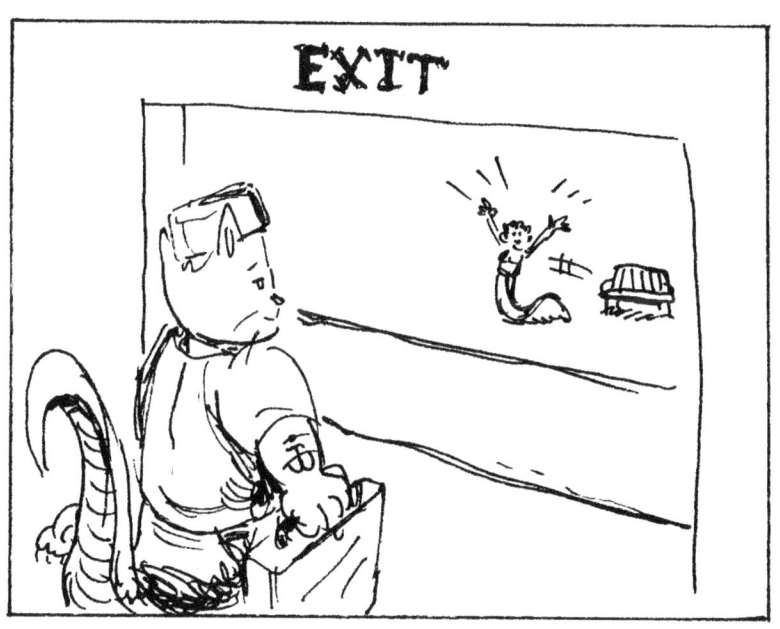

REST . . .

AH, ANNE! BLESS YAH' HEAHT!

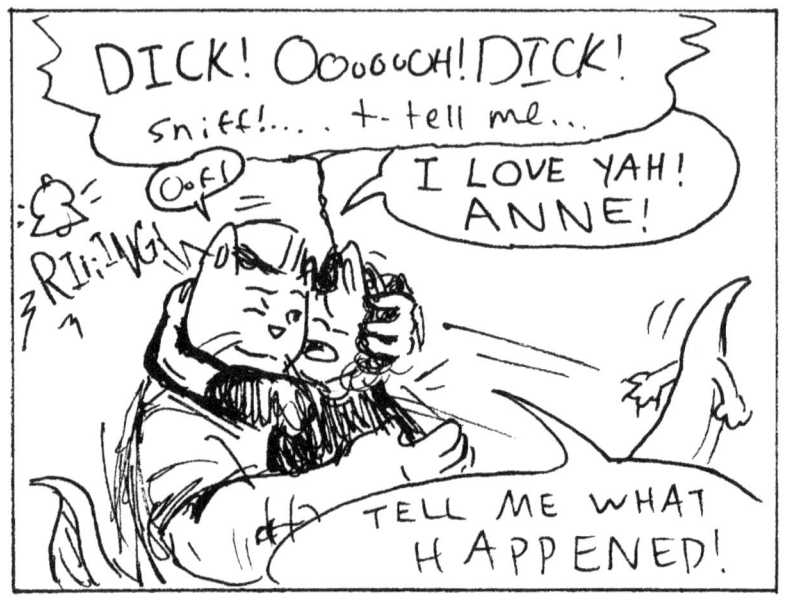

. . .

WHAT HAPPENED?

SHE MEANS. . .

NO.

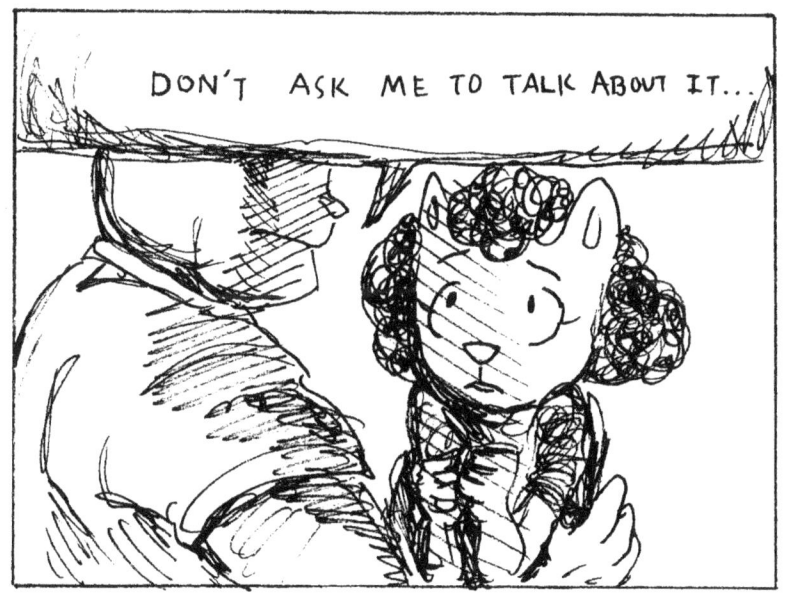

DON'T ASK ME WHAT HAPPENED,
ANNE...

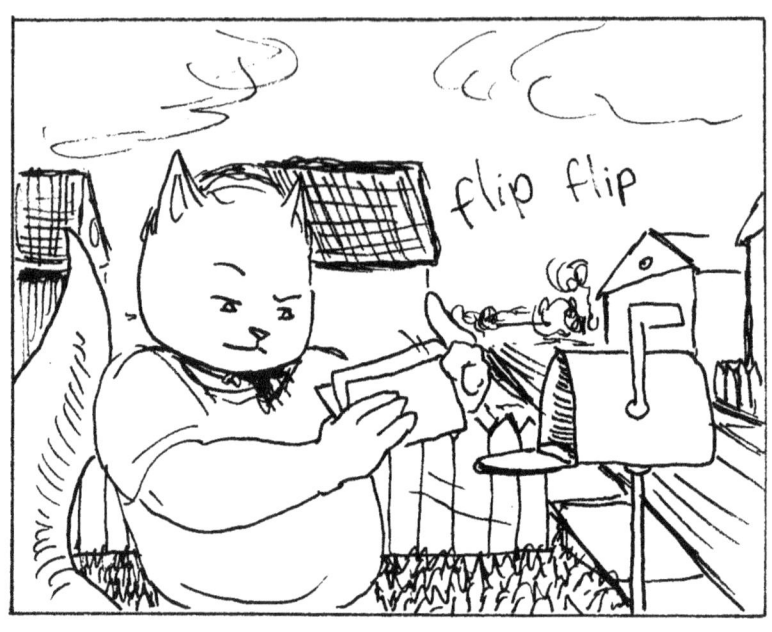

OFFICIAL LOOKIN'...

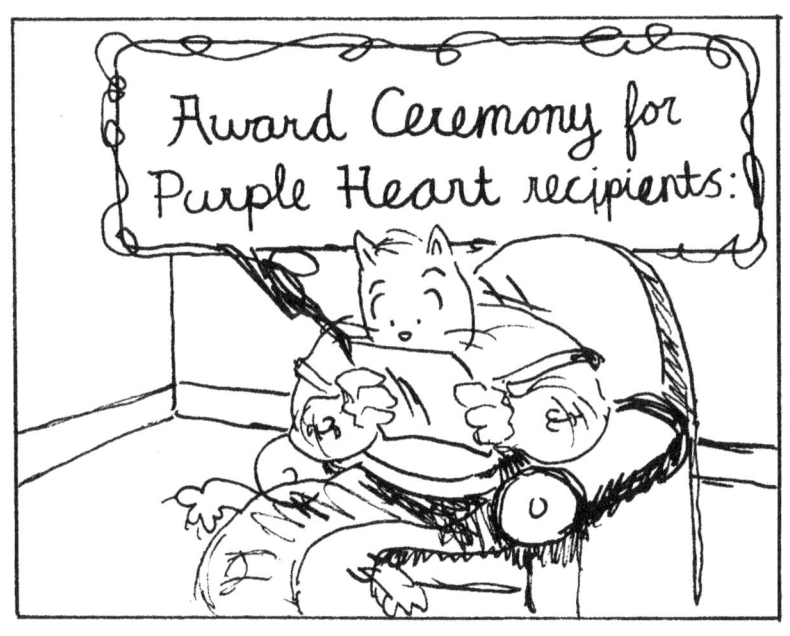

AND— !!!

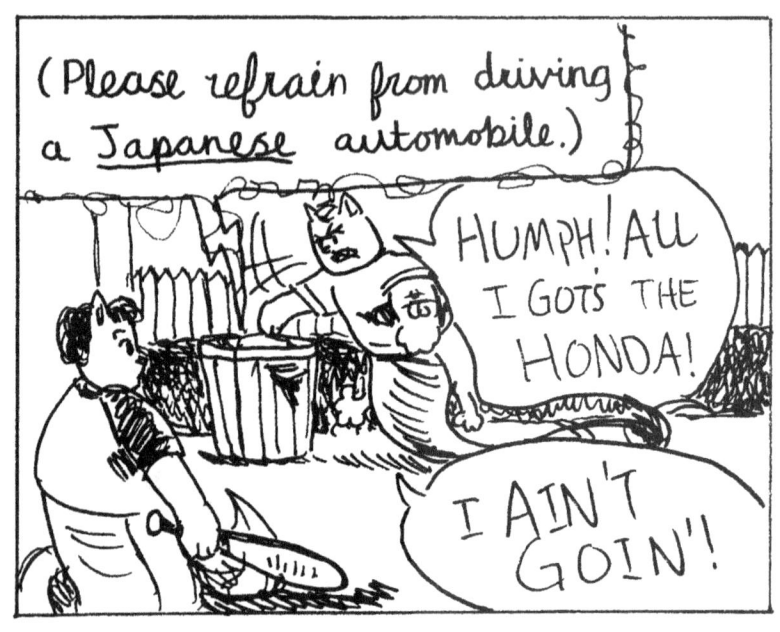

DON'T WANT TH' LOOKS!
DON'T WANT TH' QUESTIONS!

RICK IS A SMAHT KID.

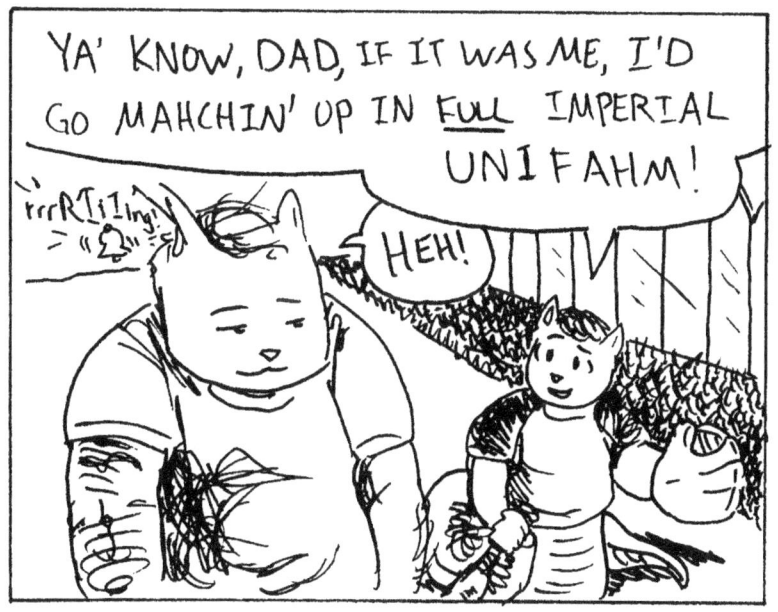

SMAHT ALECK, TOO!

I'M PROUD'A ——

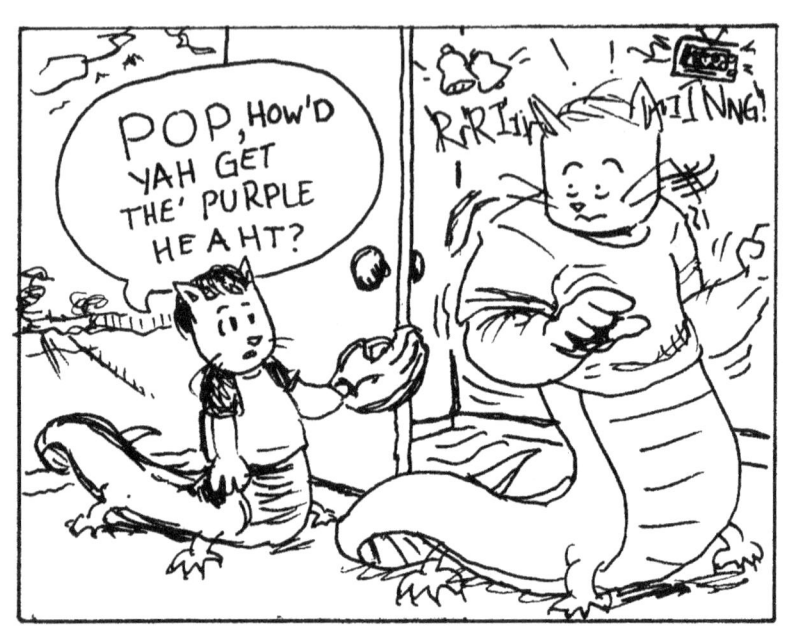

"WHAT HAPPENED"??? TUM!!! ♭!
♭!! TA!! TEE-TUM!!! LA!! DA!! —

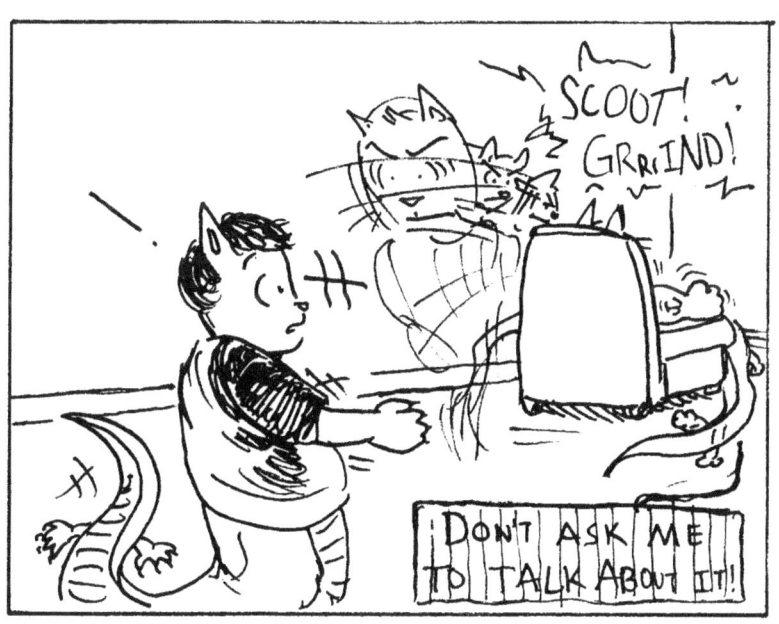

MAKE IT

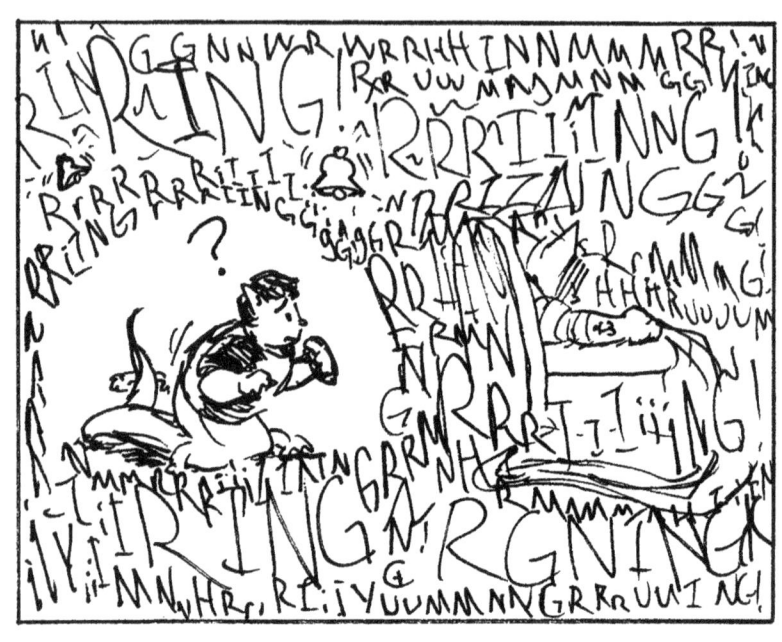

STAHP G
O AH WAY!!!
GO AH
WAYYY V!!!!!!

GONE.

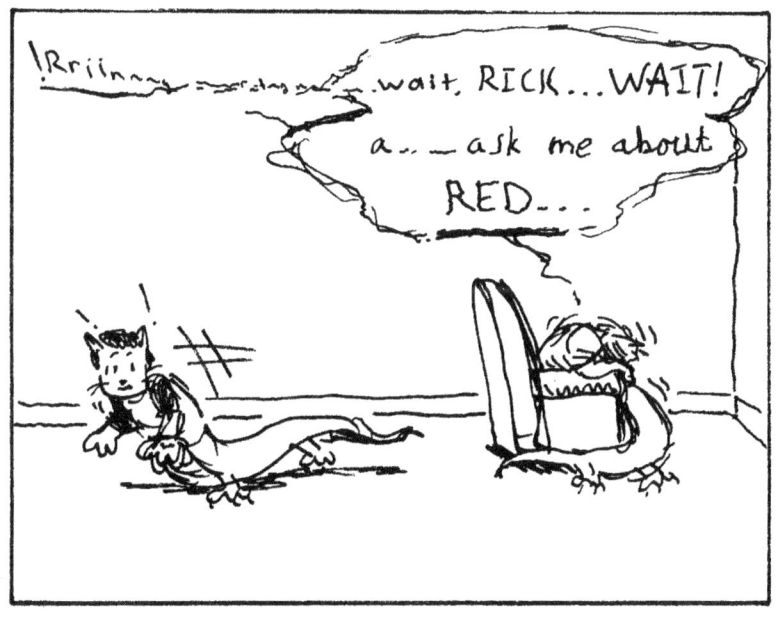

HE'S GONE.

GRADUALLY, MY STRENGTH GOES...

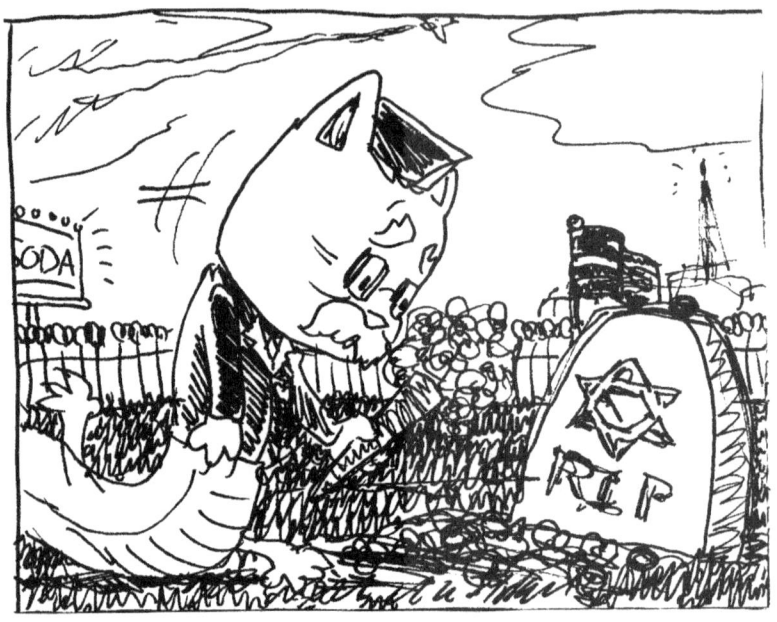

RICK'S IN LAW SCHOOL.

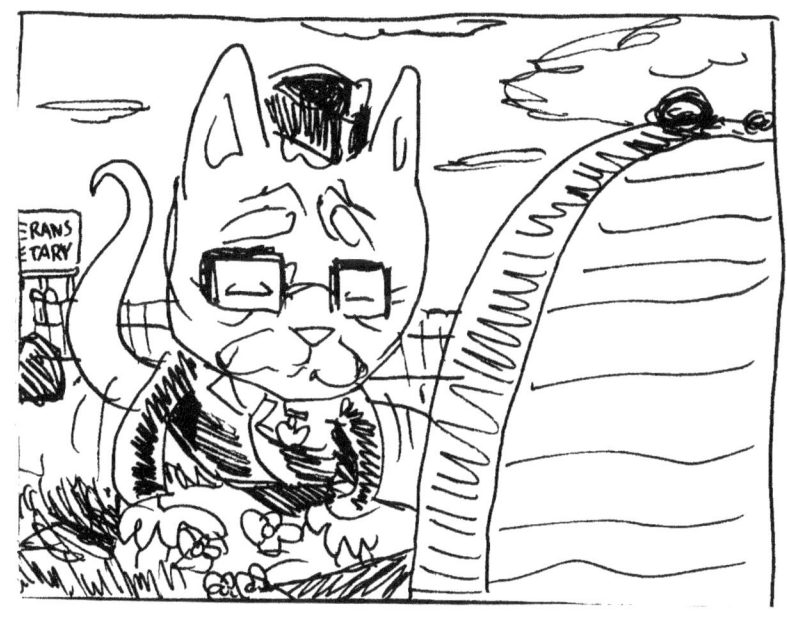

SMAHT. SUCH 'A SMAHT BOY.

LONG-HAIHED HIPPIE!

BUT ALIVE!

I THINK <u>YA'D</u> <u>HAVE</u>

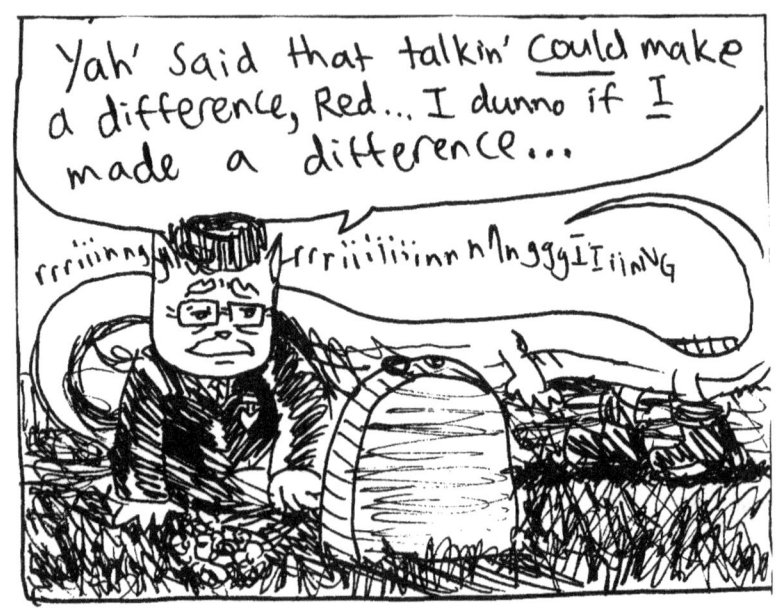

LIKED HIM? AHGUED
WIT' HIM? PUSH HIM IN
WAYS I COULDN'T? WOULD
<u>YOU</u> HAVE HAD A SON, TOO?
A DAUGHTAH?
A SMAHT GIRL?

YOU'D HAVE BEEN A SECOND

But I talked to my son about
YOU!
v

12-7-1941. "Red" died on the U.S.S. Arizona

FATHAH´

TA' MY ONLY SON...

I'D HAVE BEEN A SECOND

FATHAH´

To HOW MANY, RED?

WILL WE MEET ?

ABOUT THE AUTHA':

Smiley
BONE
BOTH
LAUGHED
AND
FELT
BAD
WHILE
WRITIN'
DIS'
COMIC.

www.ingramcontent.com/pod-product-compliance
Lightning Source LLC
Chambersburg PA
CBHW061449180526
45170CB00004B/1627